CULTIVATING PATIENCE EXPERIENCE HOPE

By Lisa S. Adamson

Copyright © 2023 by Lisa Simone Adamson

Written By: Lisa Simone Adamson

Cover Art by: Lisa Simone Adamson

Edited by: Britnie Anderson

ISBN: 978-1-7782764-2-2

Scripture quotations in this book are from the King James Version of the Bible unless otherwise identified.

This book is dedicated to:

All my precious mothers in the faith who have encouraged me in this thing called womanhood; those elder ladies who took time to speak into my life and who saw the best in me, when I had no clue;

All my precious sisters and daughters in the faith that have been a constant source of support and strength as I endeavor to walk in the pathways of those who have gone before me; and

My precious Victory

With Love

Contents

Introduction

Welcome to *"Cultivating: Patience Experience Hope"*

You are reading this right now because God is unfolding His plan for your life. His plan is to draw you closer and to nourish your soul. He knows exactly what you need.

This devotional journal was created to encourage and empower you to cultivate patience and faith in your walk with Him. Many women can relate to being overwhelmed with stress and insecurity. Often maintaining a balance between work/life/faith creates conflict that leaves you feeling drained and disconnected from your faith. This is not God's will. His desire is that you be anchored and secure. His desire is that all the strength that you need will be found in a firm faith.

The purpose of this devotional is the help you find that rootedness in God that centres you, so that you become confident and strong. You will learn how to study and dig into Gods word. There are several strategies and tips suggested as tools for the job. You must be willing to flow with the Holy Spirit and draw from His well. This book will inspire you to be strong and courageous. It will remind you of the hope that is found in the Christian faith.

It can be used as a daily or weekly bible devotion and can be done on your own or as part of a group. I suggest taking time to work through the challenges and reflection questions to really get the most out of your quiet time with God. Expect to read scriptures and think through the questions, this is where growth will happen. It is an open and shut devotional meaning that you only need your bible and this book. There is space to journal, write or diagram. Remember that this conversation is between you and your Lord!

May the Lord grant you joy and inspiration as you journey forward.

The Featured Sections

The "**Read**": This lists the scriptures that set the tone and foundation of the devotional. Read these first.

The "**Write**": This is the recommended scripture for copying into the journal. Writing the word help you to slow down and meditate on the message. It helps you to hide the word in your heart.

The "**Hope**" These are power statements that remind us of Gods promises and vision.

The "**Reflection**": This list of questions and prompts can be used for journalling and prayer.

The" **Challenge**": These help you to put Gods word into practice.

The "**Dig Deeper**": These Dig Deeper challenges are sprinkled throughout the text to help deepen your relationship with God.

Dear Lord,

As my sister is beginning this journey with You. I pray that you will overcome her with the power of your word and speak to her heart. I pray that as she works through these devotionals that she will be strengthened and encouraged by the scriptures and testimonies. Help her to carve out the time to spend with you. Open her eyes to see the beauty that you are cultivating in her day by day, through each challenge and trial. Grant her faith to believe the messages of hope, patience to wait and grace to grow. Have your way in her life and make her mountain to stand firm, for she is a vessel of worth.

Thank you for all that have done, are doing and will do.

In Jesus' majestic name.

Love your daughter,

Lisa

O Give Thanks

Read: Joshua 2:1-24, Psalms 136

Write: Psalms 136:1-4

As a mom for over 29 years, I have often been overwhelmed by all the expectations and responsibilities that I have faced in my many roles; at home, on the job, or at church. I remember, constantly parenting out of guilt and fear as a younger mom. Would I meet my children's needs? Am I enough for my husband? Am I failing at life? That was a rough way to start out womanhood and a lot of it was connected to my past and feeling unequipped.

As ladies we can sometimes become disillusioned, overwhelmed, and resentful in life, especially when we focus on ourselves. Sometimes its our past that threatens to pull us back into some place of anxiety and depression. You do not have to stay there. Think about Rahab who really did not belong, because of her background: she was a gentile and she was a "harlot." However, mercy found her and prevailed in her life. Rahab teaches us that regardless of our "past" we can be used to do great things. We can change lives; we can have an impact. Our work may seem insignificant but you are important and the work that you do has value. For this we can give thanks.

Raising children is hard, running a business is hard, homeschooling is hard, and all the many responsibilities that we have on our plates are daunting. Many of us have even battled with burn out. But I want to encourage you that His grace is present and sufficient.

God's mercy is with us every day, even when we cannot feel it. It keeps us. We are encouraged to leave everything behind and embrace His outstretched arms that promises to show us a better way. I have learned to trust that God means well for me and my family.

For I know the thoughts that I think toward you, saith the Lord, thoughts of peace, and not of evil, to give you an expected end. (Jer. 29:11)

"For we walk by faith, not by sight" 2 Cor 5:7. It is not what we see with our natural eyes, but what we see through the eyes of faith. God working. Just as He did in the beginning; His spirit moved upon the face of

the waters and spoke and there was change (Gn 1:1-3). His spirit moves upon the depths of our hearts, speaks to us, and brings changes. His presence changes you.

♥ <u>The Hope:</u> You have Gods favour in your life, and He means well.

Reflection:

1. Complete a word study on "mercy". *(Write the definition and find other scriptures about mercy)*

2. What are some of the ways God's enduring mercy has been manifested in your life?

Challenge:

Following the example of Psalms 136, continue the phrases:

To him that...

To him which...

To him who...

 Make it a personal thanksgiving and testimony.

Example:

O give thanks unto the Lord for his mercy endureth forever. To him which saved my soul from the powers of darkness and witch craft and broke the strongholds of sin.

To him who hold my life in his hands and commands every beat of my heart.

Write: Psalms 136:1-4

Beauty & Fear

Read: Proverbs 31:10-31
Write: Proverbs 31: 30-31

We are constantly bombarded with the message that we are not enough. There is something wrong with you. The beauty standards of the world can you leave you feeling depressed because it focuses on the outward man, while the inner man is neglected and undervalued. Even Samuel the prophet was tempted to anoint the next king of Israel based on external appearances.

For many years I struggled with the idea of beauty. My ideas were formed at an early age and in my opinion, I fell drastically below the beauty standards of the world and of my own community. My complexion, my shape, my hair texture was all wrong and I would struggle for years, overcompensating in many ways trying to be accepted. I relied on makeup and clothing to appear "beautiful" and neglected the inner man. I feared the opinions of people greatly. It would not be until I gave my life to Christ in my mid 20's that I would fully embrace the scriptures:

For the Lord taketh pleasure in his people: he will beautify the meek with salvation. (Psalm 149:4)

He hath made every thing beautiful in his time:(Ecclesiastes 3:11)

It would take some time, but through the washing of the Word and the renewing of my mind, I would come to embrace natural beauty and highly value the nurturing of the inner man. My fear would turn to God, who invited me to come before Him as I am. We should take time to nurture our outward man, as best as we can. A pretty dress can make you feel elegant and renewed, but there is more to you than a pretty dress.

❤ <u>The Hope:</u> You are beautiful, because you are fearfully and wonderfully made.

Here are some women of the bible that come to mind, when I think about beauty:

Deborah the Judge: She was not afraid to speak for God. She was bold and wise. She was a vessel that feared God. (Judges 4:4-9)

Jael: She was cunning. God used her to fulfill His word spoken by Deborah. She was ready and available. (Judges 4:17-22)

Mary and the Alabaster Box: She was not afraid of the naysayers, or maybe she was, but her love for Jesus was greater. She worshipped at the feet of JESUS. She was keen, bold and a worshipper. (Matthew 26:7-13)

Ruth the Moabite: She pursued God and stuck to Naomi her mother-in-law when times were rough. She was faithful, and committed (Ruth 1-4)

Esther: She obeyed Mordecai, and God used her to deliver Israel out of the hands of their enemy. She was humble and responsive. (Esther 1-10)

His presence makes you beautiful.

Reflection:

1. How does the Word of God define true beauty? Find and record a scripture that defines God's view of beauty. Why did you choose that scripture?

2. Contrast persons in the bible that exemplified internal beauty and external beauty? What were their fruits? What was the end of that person? Think about Esther and Vashti for example (Esther 1)

3. How has the fear of the Lord directed your steps? How is it different from the fear of man?

Challenge:

Dive deeper by doing a short character study on one of your favourite ladies of the bible.

Write: Proverbs 31: 30-31

One Thing

Read: Psalms 27
Write: Psalms 27:4

Many years ago, I met a lady, who was put together attractively, always well dressed, and quite sophisticated. However, her countenance did not reflect someone who had accomplished much. She was broken and discouraged.

At first, our interactions were minimal until we crossed paths in the lunch room. That would be the start of our daily walk and friendship. She shared with me that she was a mother of 5 beautiful children, she had a lovely home in a coveted Toronto neighbourhood, but she was unhappy in her marriage.

Things had crept in and it was eating away at her relationship with her husband. She tried many times to confront the situation, but it was to no avail and this left her depressed and ashamed. She had faith in God, but was not faithfully reading the word and praying. So, we set aside some of our lunch time to pray about the situation and get into the word. I cannot say that the situation changed right away, but I can testify that her countenance changed.

Despite the circumstance, she started to turn her eyes toward JESUS. Her confidence and faith in God began to rise and she realized that while she could not change her husband, she could have a personal walk with God and continue to believe Him for strength and grace. The light of that knowledge radiated through her. She became more open and confident. We would remain friends long after I moved to another role in my job.

Life's circumstances can really drain us and keep us from seeing that God is good. He is a friend that sticks closer than a brother. Sometimes situations change, sometimes they take a long time, and at other times they remain the same. Our relationship with God does not have to be contingent on our present situation. His presence is enough.

"One thing have I desired of the Lord, that will I seek after" v.4

Reflection:

1. What are some of the obstacles and challenges that you encounter in your daily pursuit of God?

2. How do you overcome them?

3. List as many synonyms that you can think for the word "determination" (if you have time add a word study)

Challenge:

Encourage someone in your circle of influence that may be struggling with establishing a spirit of determination in their pursuit of God. If you are going through a difficult time, surround yourself with sincere people that will pray, and walk through the word with you.

 In verse 18 it states: *Wait on the Lord: be of good courage, and he shall strengthen thine heart: wait, I say on the Lord.* What are you waiting on God for? Write them down. What requests or promises have you received from God? Write them down too.

Where no counsel is, the people fall: but in the multitude of counsellors there is safety (Proverbs 11:14)

Write: Psalms 27:4

Are You Ready? (Part 1)

Read: Luke 12:16-40
Write: Luke 12:21

What if you were to pass into eternity... now? Suddenly? How many people have "died before their time"? As I ponder these questions, the first thoughts that come to my mind are how would my husband and children survive? Have I prepared them enough to function without me? Have I made things right with people in my life? Will I leave a testimony? Am I ready?

Are you ready? It's a jarring and sobering thought because it reminds us that we are all appointed to leave this earth and enter into another phase of existence, eternity. With this comes the knowledge of eternal preparation.

Ready means to be fully prepared, in a suitable state for action

Life has us busy; surviving, trying to make ends meet, and accumulating goods to make life as comfortable and liveable as possible. These are goals, right? without a vision the people perish and so many of us have a vision of what a successful life looks like. If you have small children, you are probably really occupied with trying to ensure that they have a happy childhood and are well taken care of. These things keep us very occupied. However, Jesus does remind us to be rich towards God. To seek Him for the daily bread and keep an eternal perspective.

We are reminded to consider the lilies how they grow: they toil not, they spin not; (Luke 12:27). This teaches us to trust God, and be anxious for nothing. We are reminded that taking care of our soul is important. His presence is life.

♥ <u>The Hope</u>: You have an eternal destination.

Reflection:

1. How does the thought of eternity make you feel? Explore why.

2. How can you keep eternity at the forefront of your mind, without panicking or becoming anxious?

3. What do you envision eternity to look like? Is there a favourite scripture that inspires this vision? Write it down or diagram it.

Challenge:

Take some time reflects on the treasures in your life. Is there anything that you are holding unto in your heart or life that would interfere with your readiness should the Lord decide to call you home? Perhaps the Lord wants to move you into something greater in your life, but things are standing in the way. Ambitions, goals, dreams… etc. create a spiritual bucket list and start cleaning out your spiritual closet

So, teach us to number our days, that we may apply our hearts unto wisdom. (Psalm 90:12)

Write: Luke 12:21

Are You Ready? (Part 2)

Read: 2 Cor 10:3-7, Revelation 3:14-22, Luke 14:27-33
Write: 2 Cor 10:6

Words that are synonymous with ready: ripe, fit.

In Rev. 3:14-22, the Lord addresses the church at Laodicea, who is in a state of complacency "neither cold nor hot:I would that thou wert cold or hot" speaking of their lukewarmness. They have accumulated a lot of wealth and it has lulled them into a state of sleepiness, as a result, they have lost sight of the season and time. Their purpose and light has taken a back seat to their present condition.

We are reminded that we are in warfare and in order to prevail it will take commitment, steadfastness, and obedience to God's word. "For the weapon of our warfare is not carnal, but mighty through God" 2 Cor. 10:4

We need to stay ready. Carving out dedicated time to read, pray, and meditate in God's word will give us the power we need to stay alert and be ready. Like a fruit that is ripe for the picking in its season. We don't know at what minute or hour the Lord may call on us to be used in some way or some person's life. If we are too busy or preoccupied, we will miss what He is doing in the spiritual realm. Think of Jael, who was ready to move into action when the situation arose?

♥ <u>The Hope</u>: You are on a journey to a better you, filled with power and walking in victory. You are being called

There is one who seeks to devour you. Let us close that door and be ready for greatness. His presence is safety.

Reflection:

1. How does the word obedience make you feel? Examine your feelings associated with this word and attempt to find the source or origin of any negative feelings.

2. Compare and contrast the phrase grudging obedience and willing obedience? What is at the root of each? What is the fruit of each? What is the outcome?

Every man according as he purposeth in his heart, so let him give; not grudgingly, or of necessity: for God loveth a cheerful giver. (2 Cor 9:7)

3. Are there areas of your life where you are acting out in grudging obedience? Is it because of attitude/hurt, be honest with yourself and with God.

4. What is the Lord's personal challenge to you through these scriptures?

Challenge:

In order to prevail, our house must be in order! The challenge today is to take stock of your life, as we continue to look at readiness and preparedness, and examine every area and pocket of our lives. There is power in obedience even when it's uncomfortable. As we continue in this same vein of reflection in the next devotion, allow the Holy spirit to guide you in preparation for His service and work through you. Let's pause and assess so that we can rise with power to overcome and stand strong, being in readiness and fit for the Masters use!

Are You Ready? (Part 3)

Read: Luke 16:21-26, Luke 9: 61-62
Write: Luke 9: 62

Several years ago, my family and I had the opportunity to purchase a new home direct from a builder. We made our purchase based on the floor plan drawings, and chose the lot. We visited the site often just to observe the various stages, the forming of the foundation, and the framing of the structure etc. It gave us the chance to pray over it as it was being built.

Before moving in, we completed a Pre-Delivery Inspection. This allowed us to walk through each room with the Site Superintendent, to examine the workmanship and ensure that everything was built and completed soundly. To make sure its ready!

The scripture says that a wise man builds his house upon a rock and when the test comes, it stands strong because it's built on a firm foundation. The structure of the house is just as important as what the house is filled with. The rating of the insulation, the standard of the wiring, and the quality of the finishings.

Today, we are challenged to examine our temple to ensure that is not only swept and garnished but filled with the Holy Ghost which is light, truth, and power. Christ is our insulation.

Finally, my brethren, be strong in the Lord, and in the power of his might. Put on the whole armour of God, that ye may be able to stand against the wiles of the devil. Ephesians 6:10-11

Every step that we take in the kingdom of God is drawing us closer to God. Our prayers, commitments, and sacrifices, are anchoring us in the faith and building a firm foundation for today and tomorrow. His presence is wisdom.

💜 <u>The Hope:</u> Your testimony can never be erased.

What the Lord has done for you shall be permanent and established. Only keep His testimony in remembrance.

Reflection:

1. We are the temple of the Holy Ghost! How does one keep their temple secure from the enemy? List or map as many ways that come to mind. Highlight the areas that you feel need improvement in your life?

2. Landmarks. People erect physical landmarks to mark notable achievements, to keep the memory of someone alive, or to record the establishment of a community. This is chosen by one generation based on their specific ideals and criteria; however, another generation may not agree and thus remove those landmarks. Spiritual landmarks are eternal, significant, and not easily moved. They are markers and testimonies of victories and triumphs that the Lord has wrought in your life. Do you remember the day you surrendered to Christ? The day you gave up a specific vice?

Are there things that you were delivered from that are trying to creep back into your life? Has your stance or attitude changed towards these things? If so, why? Bring them before the Lord and place them on the altar!

3. Convictions & deliverance are like landmarks. What role do they play in the life of a growing Christian?

Challenge:

Examine the story of Mary Magdalene and the Demoniac over the Gadarenes, Jesus delivered these from demonic strong hold. How were their lives changed? How did JESUS use them during His ministry on earth? How are they a testimony and witness even today?

 Rejoice not against me, O mine enemy: when I fall, I shall arise; when I sit in darkness, the Lord shall be a light unto me. (Micah 7:8)

Write: Luke 9:62

Ministering to the Lord

Read: Luke 7:37-50, Matthew 26:7-13
Write: Luke 7:48-50

Counter Culture: a way of life and set of attitudes opposed to or at variance with the prevailing social norm, aka popular opinion

I recall coming into the church as a single mom with a load of guilt and shame. I had lived a life that many people twice my age had not experienced. I did not deserve to be in the house of God because of my past, I was an outsider. But, the Lord took pity on a girl who came from a dysfunctional background, was full of scars and wounds and didn't understand the language of worship and Christian etiquette. I believe this is why the story of Mary Magdalene resonates with me so deeply. When you have nothing to offer, give yourself. That is enough, that is all that Jesus wants. He will deal with the onlookers who question your position before His presence.

♥ The Hope: You are enough.

Mary did not go into the feast planning to anoint Jesus for His burial. She went to worship, to honour Him for His work in her life. It was her reasonable sacrifice.

When you worship God, obey His voice, seek His face, sing His praises, dedicate your life, are broken at His feet…you minister unto the Lord. This idea of dedication may be counterculture, which in contrast teaches us self centeredness. We are encouraged to worship ourselves instead of God.

While no one wants to walk in brokenness (it is painful, lets be honest), it does open you up to pour out all and be transparent, this is what God is looking for; a vessel that He can pour into. You do not have to come from a traumatic background to experience His presence in your life. The only requirement is to be a broken and empty vessel, like the alabaster jar. *The sacrifices of God are a broken spirit: a broken and contrite heart, O God, thou wilt not despise.* Ps 51: 17

♥ The Hope: You deserve to be in the presence of God.

Reflection:

1.   What do you think about Mary's actions towards JESUS? What do you think the alabaster jar represents?

2.   How do you feel about the actions of those around her?

3.   Define the word minister

Challenge:

Faith sometimes causes us to move counter culture especially when your earnest desire is to please God. Mordecai is another person in the bible who appeared to move counter culture due to his reverence and dedication to God.

The Bible says:

And you shall love the LORD your God with all your heart, with all your soul, with all your mind, and with all your strength.' This is the first commandment. Mark 12:30

Do you ever feel restrained or experience external pressure opposing you in your ministration unto the Lord? Take this to the Lord in prayer today. List the things that are in your heart to do for God; what is standing in the way? Speak specifically about the barriers and challenges that are attempting to drown out your personal worship, and desire to give all. Lay them down before JESUS and trust him. His presence heals us.

Write: Luke 7:48-50

Ministering to Others

Read: Isaiah 58:6-14, Matthew 25:31-40, Luke 4:18-19, John 14:12
Write: Roman 8:14

One chilly afternoon I was waiting at the bus stop with my son, who was 5 at the time, when I noticed a young lady in dark sunglasses. I was curious because it wasn't a very sunny day. I felt the Lord tell me to speak to her. I was shy but obeyed nonetheless. I had already assessed in my mind that she would not be interested in being bombarded with Christian talk. Needless to say, I did share my faith with her and she was receptive. She eventually opened up to share that she wore sunglasses to hide her eyes. She had lost it as a result of domestic violence. I am very thankful that I obeyed the Holy spirit on that day, as a young Christian in the faith. She was dealing with trauma, feeling isolated and looking for healing. She did eventually find her identity in Christ. We would become fast friends and worship together at church until she moved away to another province.

When we are led by the spirit to reach into the lives of others, whether through words or actions, we are ministering to others. We are becoming the vessels of God. His presence is grace.

♥ The Hope: You have a purpose.

Reflection:

1.	What is the burden the Lord?

2.	Where do we find strength to fulfill His burden?

3.   In Matthew, 25:31-40 The Lord uses the imagery of the sheep and the goat to describe the nations on judgement day. Why do you think he used these animals and what attributes do they have that distinguish them from one another?

4.   Our first inclination is to look at the physical needs which is necessary, however, considering the spiritual need, what might a hungry soul, a sick soul, an imprisoned soul look like? Is it always obvious? Are they only found among those who do not know JESUS Christ? People are very good at masking and creating facades, how might we tune ourselves so that we can see beyond the physical needs?

Challenge:

In 2 Cor 5:17-18 the bible says. *He has given us the ministry of reconciliation,* in your personal devotion today, ask the Lord to open your eyes to see opportunities to minister to others with boldness and confidence. Contemplate what barriers you face with fulfilling His will in this area of your life. Create a list of ways that you can impact those around you. Start with family, if that is easier.

1 King 4:1-6 The Story of Elisha and the Widow Woman – Read this scripture as though it were more than a miracle and as though it were an allegory of the Christian life. Can you see God's plan for the church emerging in this passage?

Write: Roman 8:14

Ministering to Yourself

Read: Psalms 42 & 43 (read together, as one continuous Psalm), 1 Samuel 30:6, Esther 4:16
Write: Psalm 42:11

Did you know that chapter breaks were inserted in the Bible for ease of use, however, the original text did not have the chapter breaks as we know it!

Many times when we're going through things we might feel isolated, like no one really understands. We are never alone, but we can wrestle with bouts of loneliness. When I gave birth to my premature daughter, I felt very alone. It was a tumultuous time; our family business had taken off, my husband worked long hours, we pastored a small church, my oldest son was juggling University and work, and my two youngest sons were with me. I relocated them to Toronto to be near the hospital so that I could care for my fragile baby.

It took a toll. I know that there was a church praying for my husband and I. At times it felt like my husband and I were dealing with things in isolation. It was tough. But in the wee hours of the night, when it was just the nurses, tubes, and my tired sons, I wrestled with a constant knot of anxiety in my stomach. It would take constant prayer, singing, and scripture reading to keep my strength up and encourage my family on a daily basis. I can thankfully say that the Lord brought us through.

The bible reminds us: *the Lord will command his lovingkindness in the daytime, and in the night his song shall be with me and my prayer unto the God of my life. (*Psalms 42:8)

The Psalms is a powerful book to turn to for strength. David shows us how to worship God in the night seasons.

Encourage is to give support, confidence or hope to (someone); To inspire with courage

Courage: strength in the face of pain or grief

- ♥ The Hope: You can encourage yourself in the Lord. Your needs are important too

Grief and sadness can show up in many ways and be attached to any circumstance, but is usually associated with loss. Loss of someone, loss of security, loss of hope, loss of physical strength, these are real experiences. Take time to heal, reflect and, draw virtue. Lean into God's word for the strength to "ride out the storm." We do go through things, but we have access to the comforter. He will empower you day by day. His presence comforts you.

Reflection:

1.   Sometimes we find our selves in situations that are beyond our control, like David who was under attack and faced an uprisal from his own people; or Esther who held the fate of Israel in her actions. How can we encourage ourselves to not give up? How do we keep ourselves from perishing with grief or dismay?

2.   Psalms 42:8 reminds us that the Lord is a constant presence in the lives of His saints, in the day and night seasons. What other resources does the Lord provide His saints with during times of trouble?

Challenge:

Reflect on a time when you had to encourage yourself in the Lord, what was the situation and outcome, what scriptures comforted you? write it down and let it serve as a landmark. Give Him praise for His mighty acts. If you are presently in a place where your "soul is cast down", meditate on these psalms, making it your personal prayer, and reach out to the Lord expressing your thoughts and reflecting on the goodness the Lord. Be kind and gentle with yourself. Take time to heal, rest, and recoup so that you can have strength to fight.

Wherefore I put thee in remembrance that thou stir up the gift of God, which is in thee by the putting on of my hands. For God hath not given us the spirit of fear; but of power, and of love, and of a sound mind. (2 Tim 1:6-7)

Write: Psalm 42:11

Shine Like a Star

Read: 1 Samuel 17:32-40, 2 Cor 10:12, Proverbs 3:26
Write: Proverbs 3:26

Compare: to estimate, measure or note similarity and dissimilarity between.

Confidence: the state of feeling certain about the truth of something. The feeling or belief that one can rely on someone or something; firm trust

Convictions: a firmly held belief or opinion

For many years I stumbled around in doubt and insecurity. I knew that I had gifts and talents but never the confidence to actually use them. I would have bouts of faith and energy, but then it would recede, contingent upon people's response. I would wait in the shadows, hoping someone would see me, I mean really see me and validate me. That won't always come. But when I began to worship God and put down this overwhelming need to be validated by people, I found strength and confidence in God. He began to speak to me everywhere I went. Through preaching, through scriptures, through voice notes that ladies would send to me. He showed up everywhere. I realized that my confidence and strength did not rest in what people saw in me, but in what Christ saw in me. The things that he planted and was cultivating in me, for His purpose and glory. We were made to shine; He does say that we are a light. Don't be afraid of your luminescence.

♥ <u>The Hope</u>: You are meant to shine.

This undermining of self is too complex an issue to tackle in one devotional study, but I will assure you of this, the more you lean into God despite your insecurities, mistakes, and uncertainty, the more His mercy straightens your steps. You will discover yourself at the center of His will.

Don't lose confidence when you see others prospering in their own way. God has a way and a plan that will lead you into personal victory. The anointing in your life will move in a way that is unique to the gifts and calling that is built in you by the hands of God. When we focus on the ability and tools of others, we can become weak and immobile. We grow dim. That's not the plan of God, but a tactic of the devil to stop you from moving forward. He wants to reduce your impact.

Let me put it this way, think of yourself as an instrument created to make a specific and glorious sound. A horn doesn't make the sound of a guitar nor a guitar the sound of a piano. As the breath of God is moving on you, what glorious tune or sound will you make that is uniquely yours? There in lies your unique strength. His presence empowers you.

THINK ABOUT IT: The act of comparing among ourselves can show a lack of confidence and conviction!!!

Reflection:

1.   How significant is it that David made the decision not to use Saul's armour to go to battle? How is that a witness to us?

2.   What was David's underlying strength?

3.   As a child of God, what truths can we extract from this reading? Think of as many as you can.

Challenge:

 In your devotion today consider where the Lord is taking you, the giants that you may be facing, and lean on Him knowing that He has a plan for you.

Pray that the Lord will fortify your faith in such a way that you remain confident in your convictions and resist the temptation to compare yourself with others. List your gifts and talents. How are you using them?

Write: Proverbs 3:26

Present with the Lord

Read:1 King 19: 9-12, Psalm 23:3
Write: Psalms 23:2 *(see challenge)*

Nature Study in its simplicity involves getting outside and becoming acquainted with nature, through the senses; sketching, listening, and observing. At first, I thought my children would be bored with this, however through discipline and routine they have learned to be still. They tune in to hear birds in the distance, recognize different species of birds, to identify markers of seasonal change, and ultimately see God's beauty in creation. Even now when going for a walk, they will point out a caterpillar on the side walk or a beaver dam in the woods. Now, they are the ones that draw my attention to different observations. They value the time outside strolling leisurely and will often talk about the idea of being too busy or too loud to notice details.

Noise can come in many forms. Sometimes it is extremely clamorous to the point of creating physical discomfort or chaos, at other times its various distractions, social media, responsibilities, the devil, and at other times our own voice of reason or lack thereof. It can be so overwhelming that the voice of God is lost in the multitude. Unfortunately, when we get to that state of not hearing God's voice, we can become anxious and fixated on our problems. The presence of God gives us peace. Developing a habit of seeking God, can be the element that channels his peace into your life. His presence calms you.

❤ <u>The Hope</u>: You will find God in the stillness.

Reflection:

1. What is creating noise around you today?

2. When Elijah reached out to God, it's almost like he went through phases before he heard God's voice.

3. Why did the Lord communicate with Elijah the prophet the way He did? Why is this significant?

4. What does it mean to be present?

Challenge:

Let creativity flow: Diagram Psalm 23:3 as you meditate on the Word today. Allow yourself time to be still in His presence. Attempt to press beyond the noise in your life and find the voice of the Lord. What is He laying on your heart? What is He speaking to your Spirit? Through the help of the Holy Spirit turn down the volume of distractions.

He's Already Made the Way

Read: 2 King 7:3-9, Isaiah 55:1-13, Roman 11:33, Psalms 36:6, Psalm 92:5

Write: Psalm 92:5

The Lord is good, has been good, and will always be good. Over the past 24 hours, I have just been thinking about how faithful God has been, not just in His goodness towards me, but in the keeping of His word. I am so grateful that our survival and sustenance as children of God is not dependent on anything that we could do, but solely dependent on His greatness.

Today's readings are just a reflection of all that He encompasses. We may not always understand the way He moves, but we can be confident in knowing that He is in control, and He has already made the way!!

If the Lepers did not decide to move forward, the Lord could have used somebody else or brought deliverance through some other way. The word was already spoken by the man of God (2 Ki 7:1) and God's word never goes back to Him void. It's like the snow that comes down and waters the ground. It has purpose and power. The 10 lepers unknowingly, in their own desperation and faith fulfilled the Word of God. They were a part of the plan. In the book of Esther, Mordecai reminds Esther that if she held her peace deliverance might arise from somewhere else (Esth 4:14), so we know that once God's plan is in motion it will be finished. She was part of the plan.

♥ The Hope: You are a part of the plan.

These lepers that were the outcast of society, usually left to beg and fend for themselves because of their uncleanness, became the vessels of deliverance. The Lord truly uses the weak things of the world to confound the wise (1 Cor 1:27-28)

♥ The Hope: You are not insignificant.

The extent of their desperation created the circumstance in which, nothing was left but faith. Stay and die or go and find life. Occasionally, it is in those desperate places that are void of hope and filled with helplessness, that we can see faith begin to bud. I am grateful that Jesus is the author and finisher of our faith. (Heb 12:2)

Your faith is being designed by Him. His presence is clarity.

Reflection:

1. As a child of God, how has the Lord used your desperation to move you forward into His perfect will?

2. What do these scriptures tell us about our God?

Challenge:

In your personal devotion today give thanks for all the things that He has done and is doing, things seen and unseen, things past, present and future. Let your dwelling place both physical and spiritual; be filled with thanksgiving unto JESUS.

Write: Psalm 92:5

Heart to Heart with JESUS

Read: Songs of Solomon: 5, Psalms 4:8,
Write: Psalms 4:8

When I walk into a room, my daughter almost always invariably responds. If she's sleeping, she stirs, if she's playing, she will usually stop (for a moment).

I remember when visiting her in the NICU, as soon as I would enter the room, the nurses would say "She knows her mama's here" and my daughter would confirm with open eyes and by turning her head in my direction, with tubes and masks everywhere. She could sense my presence from afar. Even today. It amazes me. I believe that there is a deep connection that cannot be defined in words, a quiet reassurance that you are loved, and, a part of something greater than yourself. You're protected and you're safe!

It makes me think about our own relationship and response to God. When we gather in praise and worship, its easier to tune into the spirit, as we collectively give our self to the spirit, and lay down the distractions, but what about our response in our day to day? Are you able to follow His scent and aroma drawing you into deeper places? His presence is sweet.

♥ _The Hope:_ You were made to hear His voice

Reflection:

1. In Song of Solomon, what stirs the heart of the speaker?

2. In the last line of Song of Solomon, how does the speaker describe the one they pursue?

3. What is the theme of this passage?

Challenge:

With all the news and media reports about death, viruses, global climate change; the list is endless, we can easily fall out of tune with the spirit. Before going about your day, or before closing your day, take time to tune into the spirit.

Try not to release from prayer or devotion today, without hearing what the spirit has to say to you. Like trying to tune into your favourite radio station, keep adjusting the dial until you can hear clearly.

Draw a large heart in your journal, jot down as many words that you can think of that describe things you may be feeling i.e., anxiety, fear, stress, …the point of this exercise is to identify some of the issues of the heart

Next, for each word in your heart, find an antonym i.e., for anxiety – peace of God and so forth and create a list. Bring these before the Lord in prayer.

Write: Psalms 4:8

The Be Attitudes (Part 1)

Read: Matthew 5: 1:12, 21-24
Write: Matthew 5:8

They say that in order to get a full "picture" of an object, it's best to sketch it from different angles. For example drawing a top view of a building, a bottom view, side view, and internal layout. These are renderings. This allows one to create a visual representation while analyzing it from different vantage points. I recently tested this out, one evening, while sketching a pine cone. As I practiced this, I realized that by the time I got to my third sketch of the pine cone, I was adding more detail and dimension. It actually works. When studying the word it's also helps to compare the stories and scriptures with scriptures. It sometimes adds dimension to understanding the words of Christ. We will do this over the next two devotional studies.

Search the Scriptures; for in them ye think ye have eternal life: and they are they which testify of me. (John 5:39)

In Matthew 5, the Lord lays down some key foundational truths on the Christian attitude and posture before Him and in this world. Tied to the attitudes are eternal blessings. It reminds me of Deuteronomy 11 where God sets out the conditions of blessings and cursing before the children of Israel in the wilderness. In cultivating these attitudes in our daily lives, along with His grace and mercy, we are able to keep His commandments. Think about the 10 commandments as you reflect on these scriptures. While we could not keep the law by the flesh, through Him we are empowered to live by the spirit!!

Many times, we are pressed because of our faith and belief, especially when we insist on following the Word of God. People have a tendency to disdain what they don't understand or what they themselves don't have the strength to do. Like taking a stance for what is right or withdrawing from what they know to be evil. Years ago, my husband and I decided that we did not want a TV in our home, for us the benefits did not outweigh the cost. We noticed that with limited access to TV or cable, the children were more creative and imaginative. This did not sit well with our immediate family and we were labelled as radical and our children treated as though they were poor. Fast forward to today and with the changes in society, all the subtle and overt indoctrination, our families have slowly realized that our children are blessed and protected. Insulated, not isolated. It took some years of having to defend our position, especially at family gatherings, but now as our children are growing socially, confident, articulate, and creative, they see the benefits of the kingdom of God. There are times when you must "come out from among them" even when it's the people you've known all your life. We again encountered this when we decided home-schooling, every school year, we had to launch a defence. But as Matthew 5 teaches us, we are blessed.

Jesus said" Blessed are you, when men shall revile you, and say all manner of evil against you falsely for my sake (Matthew 5:11) ….and again for "righteousness' sake" in verse 10

♥ <u>The Hope:</u> You are blessed when you stand firm.

Reflection:

1.   If you were to choose a scripture from this passage as encapsulating the central theme or message which one(s) would it be? Why?

Challenge:

Ask the Lord to highlight any areas that is keeping you from transforming into the posture that He wants for you. Note these areas in your journal, as these can help you to shape a new vision for your walk with God. In His presence is strength.

Analyse the story of Joseph via the Beatitudes. How does he demonstrate the attitudes?

Write: Matthew 5:8

The Be Attitudes (Part 2)

Read: Matthew 5: 1:12, Luke 6:17-36
Write: Psalms: 34:19

As I reflect on the scriptures in today's readings, I am reminded of Matthew 7:*14 strait is the gate, and narrow is the way, which leadeth unto life, and few there be that find it.*

We are called with a high calling of grace and truth, and there really is no provision for the fleshly attitudes. Though we may falter and fall, there is an expectation that we get back up again.

For a just man falleth seven times, and riseth up again: but the wicked shall fall in into mischief (Proverbs 24:16 KJV).

We rise, not by our own strength, but by reliance on God, understanding that the things of the world are not able to sustain us because they are temporal. We can make ourselves rich, not referring to financial wealth only, but so over taken with the pleasures of life, that we ourselves despise Christ. To remain close to Christ and deny ourselves of the things that are indulgent is to be poor, to adhere to His word, which separates us from the crowd is to remain poor, it opens us up to criticism, despisings and persecutions. However, there are blessings in that. There is insight and wisdom, there is eternal wealth that is not recognized in the carnal realm. There is relationship with our saviour. Through scripture we are invited to walk as JESUS walked, Him being the master, and we, His servants. The servant is not greater than his lord (John 15:20).

Jesus was persecuted and called a devil, even though he performed miracles that had never been done before, so we endure the same sentiments. Repeatedly, JESUS advised the Pharisees that his works speak for themselves, yet the confrontation of the light in the face of the darkness, was too great and it stirred up the things, attitudes and sentiments that were hidden in the heart. Its is easy to bury ourselves, our gifts, our calling, the light; in essence, to avoid the tension and discomfort of persecution. That is the temptation JESUS assures us that he has not only overcome, but he has prayed for us.

The Hope: You are a light.

We do often suffer for our faith and desire to fulfill the Word of God. Not much different from those historical figures who have endeavored to press against the status quo, at risk of peril, to be a light. To forge a better way for humanity. *And ye shall be hated of all men for my names sake: but he that shall endure to the end the same shall be saved* (Mark 13:13). If we refuse to question the things that are evil, we will fall prey to them and our children will suffer all the more.

In these scriptures, the Lord sets before us the blessings and the woes. Teaching us the benefits and the consequences of living a sacrificial life. We can take comfort that we are not alone.

> *Be sober, be vigilant because your adversary the devil, as a roaring lion, walketh about, seeking whom he may devour: whom resist steadfast in the faith, knowing that the same afflictions are accomplished in your brethren that are in the world.* (1 Peter 5:8-9)

As scripture states; many are the affliction of the righteous, but the Lord delivers out of them all. In His presence is confidence.

♥ <u>The Hope</u>: You were made to be victorious.

Reflection:

1. What do you find to be the most difficult part about living for God?

2. How can these difficulties make you stronger?

Challenge:

In your time of journalling and reflection, contemplate on how reading Luke 6:17-36 helps to highlight JESUS message on the Beatitudes?

Write: Psalms: 34:19

And Again, I say, UNITY!

Read: 1 Corinthians 1:1-18, Proverbs 27:17, Ecclesiastes 4:9-12, John 13:
34-35

Write: 1 Corinthians 1:10

Unity is a theme that reoccurs in the bible repeatedly. There is something powerful that happens when a group of people can become one voice and one unit, laying aside every difference and weight. People unify for many causes, both good and bad, and in doing so, become a force to be reckoned with. They manage to affect change in instances where it would have been impossible as an individual. What more the children of God joined by His Spirit. When facing Goliath, David said "Is there not a cause?" That sounds like a rallying cry to awake and defeat the enemies of God; like fear and disunity. The enemy's desire is to fragment the people of God, whether in the home, church, or on the job: to isolate them from each other and from God, through whatever means. Think of how melodious and soothing it sounds when the worship team harmonizes and the church joins in. How powerful and uplifting is that session of worship. Voices and hearts are lifted into a realm of faith that touches heaven and connects us with God. We become acutely aware of God's majesty. Troubles vanish, and darkness flees.

♥ <u>The Hope</u>: You were made to worship in the body of Christ.

Although a much talked about topic, I do not think we will ever stop working on building unity until the Lord comes. In fact, much of the persecution that we face may be the conditions that will help us to perfect unity the way JESUS wants it to be. We have our concepts, but He who is greater has His expectations. We all need to come into alignment with God's word and realize that:

    a. There is a battle raging, now is not the time to be catatonic in our faith.

    b. In order to be victorious, we need unity; and

    c. Any great movement that has affected change has been united, persistent, and focused

Who hath ears to hear, let him hear! In His presence is fire.

1.   What was the source of division among the Corinthians? How does this parallel with believers today?

2.   What are some of the things that are holding the church back? Create a list

3.   What are the ramifications of disunity in the body of Christ? in the local assembly? In a marriage? In the home? What impact does this have on Christianity or the individual Christian?

4.	How can we contribute to the building of unity? What actions are you taking personally?

Challenge:

 Pray for unity in the body of Christ, be specific using the list of barriers identified in question #2, not just in the local assembly but worldwide, also take this time to reflect on sources of disunity that may be apparent in your own home and through the power of the Holy Ghost, cast them down. I encourage you to join with a prayer partner and seek the Lord together. Connect with someone that you know will seek the Lord earnestly, that you many sharpen one another.

The Lord is coming back for a church, a bride without spot or wrinkle.

That he might present it to himself a glorious church, not having spot, or wrinkle, or any such thing; but that it should be holy and without blemish. Eph 5:27

And the Spirit and the bride say, Come.

Read: Esther 2: 8-12, Joel 2:15-17, Isaiah 61:10-11, Revelation 21:21
Write: Psalms 93:1

As we are waiting on the Lord, not to return to normalcy after the pandemic, but for direction on His will, plan, and purpose in the church in this hour, how are we preparing ourselves? Today, I would like to turn our attention to an important and upcoming event. The marriage supper. Think for a moment about the excitement of a pending marriage? The butterflies, the wonder, the preparation, the feeling of excitement or the trepidation as you wait to finally be forever connected to your soul mate? The one you have been longing for.

I'll let you in on a little secret. One of the things I did while waiting, was to spend a lot of time praying and reading Christian books on marriage and womanhood. I wanted to be ready. Although there isn't a book that can perfectly predict all the challenges and nuances of a marriage relationship, they can provide you with some principals and insights. That season of preparation was instrumental in helping me to confront negative attitudes and misconceptions I had learned from unhealthy examples in my childhood. It was a dedicated time for me to soak in God's sweet presence and wisdom. I confronted so many emotions, but I knew what I wanted and I wasn't backing out.

Presently, the world is in a holding pattern like an airplane circling endlessly waiting for permission to land, and while we are holding, anarchy is mounting. What about the church? The bible tells us that the Lord is like a bridegroom and we are the……. (You fill in the blank). Therefore, now is the time to prepare. During this time of uncertainty, one thing is sure, Christ is coming for a bride. Now is the time to soak in His word, to be changed by His presences to be renewed by the beauty of His truth and to keep ourselves robed in white. We need to get dressed for this impending banquet. In His presence is holiness.

❤ <u>The Hope</u>: You are a part of the bride.

Reflection:

1. How does Esther's preparation to meet the King parallel the Christian life?

2. How are you preparing yourself for the marriage?

3. I know that we are in a very sober moment, however the bible says that:
   The voice of rejoicing and salvation is in the tabernacles of the righteous: the right hand of the Lord doeth valiantly. Ps 118:15
   How can there be rejoicing in our tabernacle?

Challenge:

Imagine or remember the joy in preparing for a wedding or in preparing for a significant event. Now translate that joy into your life, through scripture.

For example:

I remember searching for a dress that would be flattering, modest, beautiful, white –the scripture that comes to mind is:

I will greatly rejoice in the LORD, my soul shall be joyful in my God; for he hath clothed me with the garments of salvation, Isa 61:10, or

Searching for the perfect suit: *The LORD reigneth, he is clothed with majesty; the LORD is clothed with strength, wherewith he hath girded himself: the world also is stablished, that it cannot be moved.* Ps 93:1

Write: Psalms 93:1

That Trumpet Sound

Read: Rev 1:10-11, Rev 8:1-10, 1 Cor 15:52
Write: Matthew: 13:43

A teacher walks into a classroom; she is extremely frustrated and on the brink of tears. The classroom is rambunctious, loud, and ignoring her presence as it has been every morning for months. The students barely realize she is standing at the front of the class, of course there are a few students that are quietly and patiently sitting at their desks with somewhat pained expressions on their faces, however the majority of the students are yelling, talking incessantly, texting and cursing. On this particular morning, after much deliberation the teacher reaches into her bag and carefully pulls out a brass apparatus, as she slowly raises it to her mouth, she draws in a deep breath and finally blows with all her might. The sound fills the room and resonates throughout the hallways. The atmosphere changes. The quiet ones stood up in response, the attention of most of the students is won, of course there are a few students who now sit dejected angrily texting complaints to their parents, while others snicker and scoff. Welcome to Chaos high school where the motto is We Only Reject Law & Discipline a.k.a WORLD…pause.

This story is a fictional allegory of humanities response to the voice, presence, and authority of Jesus Christ. As the Lord sounds the trumpet, some will recognize the voice and gestures of their Lord, some will hear Him for the first time and yet others will seek out other voices as a means to stop what God is doing and silence His voice. But we know! The bible admonishes us not to harden our hearts as in the day of provocation. We need to recognize His voice and discern the atmospheric shift.

It is challenging to hear God above the many voices that bombard our minds. So many things vie for our attention, attempting to distract us. God has called us to listen, through circumstances he attempts to make us aware that He is in the room with plans to lead us into safety and rest. In His presence is knowledge.

- ♥ <u>The Hope</u>: You are being called.

Reflection:

1. What does it mean to hear the voice of God?

2. What does it mean to listen?

3. How is God trying to get your attention? What is His message to you today?

Challenge:

In your time of devotion today, I would like to challenge you to research and meditate on the references and purpose of the trumpet in the word of God. What is your take away? Write the scripture that is most meaningful to you or that speaks to your heart. The one that resonates.

Who hath ears to hear, let him hear!

Write: Matthew: 13:43

Positioned

Read: 1 King 13:1-28, 1 Chronicles 4:9,10
Write: Joshua 24:15

Position: relative place, situation, or standing

Today's reading, is a cautionary tale about a failed mission. The prophet's name is not mentioned but his story is recorded. When we are introduced to him, he is on an important assignment, manifesting his calling. He is on a mission to do the work of God. He was commissioned to cry against the city and in essence curse them. He was to shake the dust off because of God's judgement. He had a specific work and task. Not shortly thereafter, he disobeyed the word of God, not understanding his position and the authority that was invested in him. This became his downfall. He ate where he was forbidden, even though he had already done the work. He only had to leave the city to hear "well done" and perhaps receive his next mission but he was subverted and thus he died in shame.

We also are called to be set apart to serve God, to be a voice and to move with purpose. We should not allow anyone or anything to draw us away from the convictions that the Lord has spoken to you, even if you have to walk alone. The devil is a liar and deceiver. His sole mission is to stop and destroy you and he will use anything or anyone.

❤ The Hope: You are on Gods mission.

Many will see the work of God in your life and not understand, and thus distract you or become a stumbling block or even worse draw you away. Your job is to stay in tune with Gods will in your life. You can complete your mission and fulfill your purpose.

❤ The Hope: You are a woman of God.

There are many things that can delay our growth, like an unhealthy fear of people, or lack of commitment. Resist anything that threatens to tamper with God's will and plan for your life. As a mom, I've learned that children mature at different rates and so for fear of them destroying themselves, I don't give them more responsibility than they can handle, think of; teens driving, need I say more? He also will not give us more that we cannot handle.

Considered, for a moment the fact that He is working all things together for our good and that where we are may not actually be a cataclysmic accident, but his perfect will. Sadness and depression can settle into our lives when we hyperfocus on the things that we cannot control. Trust and obey. In His presence is security.

Reflection:

1. Sometimes people are the obstacles and many times it is the thoughts that we wrestle with. "I can't do this", "I will fail" or "I will be a laughingstock", what are the thoughts that you are wrestling with? Apply God's truth to these negative thoughts. Remember the enemy used Gods word to cause Eve to doubt. Same tactic different day, do not succumb to his ploy.

Challenge:

Think about Daniel's trial in the lion's den or Esther's life with the king. What was their situation and position? How were they positioned to glorify God? As you go before the Lord in prayer, ask him to examine you and prepare you for where He plans to take you; both the battle and the blessings.

Write: Joshua 24:15

Fresh

Read: Exodus 16:19-21, Lamentation 3: 22-23, Psalms 63:1, 143:8
Write: John 6:68

While we have been blessed with the modern conveniences of the fridge and freezer to help preserve and keep our food longer, most things are tastiest and best eaten fresh. Fresh baked bread does not last long at my house, it is eaten in minutes. Cool running water, on a long hot day; absolutely beautiful, a relaxing shower after an intense work out; soothing, the sound of a gentle spring on a nice afternoon walk; peaceful, the Word of God to a hungry soul; refreshing. Think about the newness of life in Christ, the ease and comfort, refreshing and renewal that comes from drinking at the fountain of life. There is something precious about a new day and new mercies.

Binge eating may satisfy temporarily, but will not take us very far. Could you imagine eating all your meals for the week on one day. If you survived, the old familiar feeling of hunger would present itself again; in at least a day or two. What about our souls, binge eating on a Sunday is not enough to sustain us for daily living. It's not God's plan. We were created with an appetite that constantly renews. We were created with rhythm, a time to eat, a time to digest, a time to burn energy, a time to sleep etc. There is a temptation to binge read, binge pray, or binge worship, which reflects our culture. It is a phenomenon where we try to consume as much as we can under the guise of convenience and time management. This can amend our behaviour and approach to the faith. Rather than having a steady dose of the word that we digest and absorb, we cram when the opportunity arises. Just like we may binge watch shows, because we have procured some downtime. It is convenient but not necessarily healthy.

Jesus prayed: Give us this day our daily bread, reminding us that we need fresh manna every day, to nourish our spiritual man and provide new strength for the day. The Word of God equips the spiritual man with new power to walk every day. In His presence there is anointing.

❤ <u>The Hope</u>: You deserve a fresh word.

1.   When is the last time that you received a fresh Word from God that spoke directly to your heart? (You know, the type of Word, that makes you want to highlight, underline, and circle scripture in your bible?)

2.   Why did Moses instruct the children of Israel not to keep Manna overnight? What was the Lord trying to teach them? What does it mean for you and me today?

Challenge:

In your alone time with God, seek for a fresh Word from God to nourish your soul. Ask the Lord to create in you an appetite and ear for His fresh word anew everyday! If you have not already, look at ways you can implement a regular time to spend in God's word and presence.

Dig deeper:

Try mind mapping the word "Fresh."

So far, I have come up with:

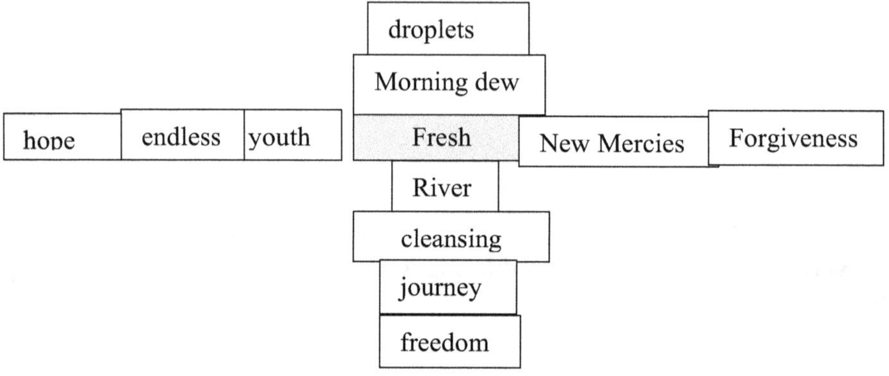

Write: John 6:68

Responding in a Changing World

Read: 2 Samuel 23:14-17, 2 King 4:12-37
Write: 2 Timothy 1:12

Think about the word "movement" as you read today's devotional.

Movement: an act of changing physical location or position or of having changed.

I want to encourage us to pause and reflect on a very simple thought; moving in response. The weight of the pandemic and events can make us feel powerless and restricted, especially with the new norms and mandates that have been emerging. It has impacted our day-to-day life and perspectives; the way we socialize and interact with others, how we travel, how we do school, work, and how we live. However, the bible reminds us that we are free in Jesus Christ. We have options, we can choose; to praise him or be frustrated, to be fearful or brave, to live or die, to be locked in our minds or free.

Let's consider David's soldiers. They were brave. Circumstances did not stop them from doing what they believed to be right, granted as soldiers that may have somewhat enjoyed the sport and challenge. The Word describes them as mighty men. They were risk takers. They teach us that nothing should stop our praise and worship; nothing should stop us from serving God. Not even a host of enemies. We can fight to get to that fountain of living water, by any means necessary.

Let also consider the Shunammite woman. She did not let death stop her from seeking God and pursuing an answer. Imagine that, death that is so final that Martha stated" I know that he shall rise again in the resurrection at the last day", when speaking to Jesus about Lazarus (Jn11:24). The Shunammite woman held her peace, did not panic, and focused on finding the healer. She did not send servants or her husband, but was determined to go herself. She reminds us that we have access to God and we can choose how we respond, how we move when confronted with adversity.

I realize that we have a fierce opponent, an adversary who is always looking for our demise, he attempts to stand in our way and cut off our connection to things faithful, but we also have a magnificent advocate who

~ 72 ~

is fighting for us and conquering the darkness. At times when I have felt my lowest, I have shifted my perspective to the wonder of God's love and protection that has given me the strength to fight. Greater is He that is in you than he that is in the world. That word is truth and will always remain true. Let this move you to respond in faith every time. In His presence there is hope.

- ♥ <u>The Hope</u>: You determine how you respond

Reflection:

1. In 2 Samuel 23:14-17 considering the situation, what impressions do you get of the men in this story? How might this apply to us spiritually?

2. In 2 King 4:12-37 how does the Shunnamite witness to us?

3. What choices can you make today to help you move forward or get on track in a way that helps you to be whole physically, mentally, spiritually?

Challenge:

In your time of personal reflection and prayer, take a closer look at how you are responding to the present situation. Have you allowed things to fall to the wayside, or become neglected as an attempt to manage during this time of crisis? When my daughter was in the NICU, I remember the nurses sharing with me that in critical times the body will allocate resources to the most important organs first (the brain and heart) as a survival mechanism at the cost of other organ functions, which in the normal scheme of things are essential but deemed not essential during crisis. Do you have an exit strategy? When things become overwhelming or difficult are there scriptures that you rely on? Write them down.

Dig Deeper:

How does the topic of choices and movement play out in the story of Paul and Silas. How might their story have been different if they responded differently? Our praise may be a catalyst for change.

Write: 2 Timothy 1:12

He Keeps Us

Read: 2 Timothy 1: 7-15, Luke 5:36-39, Psalms: 121:5
Write: 2 Timothy 1:13-14

Be encouraged, the Lord knows what He is doing, and what path each of us is on. He is able to keep us.

There are continual themes throughout the bible i.e. purpose, vision, calling, adversity, triumph, and unity (as mentioned in one of our previous devotions); they all seem to be interwoven. He has always been God throughout each situation and He is still God today. We have the new wine (the anointing), which not only keeps us but also gives us the strength to face each day! We become empowered, wiser, stronger, and deeper as we allow the spirit to abide in us, to cure in us, as wine in new bottles. With Jesus in the vessel, we can smile at the storm. He gives us the ability. We do not have to be ashamed of the faith; it is the faith that keeps us.

♥ <u>The Hope</u>: You are kept by the Word.

There are times when living for God is easy and then there are those circumstances where you are confronted with trouble, real life adversities that tests your faith. As I recall the birth and journey of my micro preemie, I remember the intense feeling of fear with each medical report that always presented the worst-case scenario. It was heart breaking and very stressful. I had to decide to believe that God was going to keep us. As a demonstration of my faith in God's word, I wrote down a scripture for every prognosis the doctor gave me and made them my prayer points. This became my daily ritual and helped me to wait on the God that was keeping me.

In my opinion, JESUS is the real super hero. He died and rose again; He performed miracles and is still doing it today. I think the storyline of super heroes in the comics that never die, are inspired by the "real" champion; Our Lord is not only able to keep us, but promises to raise us up in the last day. JESUS is our reality. His word continues to stand the test of time, and as we rest in His word and let us live in his, we are sustained. In His presences there is protection.

Reflection:

1. What does the Apostle Paul say our Saviour Jesus Christ has accomplished in this world? (Verse 10 – pretty powerful)

2. What keeps us back from committing everything into God's hands?

Challenge:

As you reflect in your time of prayer, acknowledge the Lords keeping power and commit everything into His hands, your present and your future. The Lord will preserve you through His word and will sustain you and your family in preparation for tomorrow. I have literally prayed "Lord, give us this daily bread", in a time of need and He has repeatedly provided.

If you are feeling creative, create something to help you encapsulate the message in Psalms 121

Write: 2 Timothy 1:13-14

Consistency

Read: Luke 18:1-9
Write: 1 Corinthians 15:58

consistency: a steadfast adherent to the same principle, cause or goal

Many years ago, my husband and I decided to renovate our basement. We wanted to create a space for worship and fellowship. As a result, we stripped everything down to the fiberglass and concrete floors. When we removed the old kitchen counter, we noticed a divot in the concrete floor, under our waters main shut off valve. The water had been quietly dripping in that one spot for over a long period and started creating a hole in the foundation. The consistent and constant drip drop of water impacted the solid concrete foundation.

The parable of the unjust judge shows us just how persistence and consistence are effective. In this instance, the judges' mind was changed, though he "feared not God or man" and the Lord also states that he will avenge His elect when they "cry day and night".

This year's theme in my life has been consistency. There were so many changes that I wanted to see in my life, family, and homeschool. Once I made this the motivation and focus, I found myself, developing plans and then attacking them through, regular prayer and tasks. I have seen a tremendous shift in my life by applying this principle of consistency. It was not always easy or without opposition, but consistency provided me with a path to vision. It provided me with a baseline. Things that seemed really daunting became doable. I wrote and published my first children's book and I am currently working on another. My homeschool has become much more structured, manageable, and predictable. Consistency is powerful.

♥ <u>The Hope</u>: Your consistency will pay off.

What does consistency look like in the life of a Christian?

- It is the intentional building of a prayer and worship life,
- It is a life of surrender and dedication,
- It is maintaining the same mind towards God regardless of the circumstances (think about the three Hebrew boys)

What are the benefits of consistency?

- It helps us to build a solid foundation (Matthew 7:24)
- if we keep the word of God and the testimonies of God then we will be established "for evermore"
- the word of God will create a foundation for us and for future generation (Psalm 132:12)
- We build a strong relationship with Christ and are able to stand based on what we've experienced and our testimonies become spiritual landmarks. We are even able to war in the spirit when we've gain victory in certain areas of our life. This equips us to pray and be empathetic with others. (Psalms112:6)
- Strength for times of weakness and trial: the time we spend in prayer is valuable time before the Lord building our relationship and investing in the Kingdom of God (Galatian 6:9)
- Helps to establish momentum, building a force and faith that helps us to move forward

Reflection:

1. How has consistency benefited your walk with God? Is there room for improvement?

Challenges:

 What daunting task have you been wrestling with? What visons have been laid on your heart? Create a list. This will become your game plan. Brainstorm what tasks you need to do to get there. Draft a plan. Pray over them. Revise. Be consistent. In His presence there is power to fight.

Write: 1 Corinthians 15:58

Momentum

Read: Genesis: 41, Exodus 43:27-35
Write: Proverbs 18:15

Momentum: the force that keeps an object moving after it has started; the force or speed of an object in motion

Through consistency, you can begin to develop of sense of momentum. This momentum keeps things powering forward, even when obstacles threaten to stop you. The power that you have cultivated through regular seeking and knocking manifests as the force and will to overcome. This is the manifestation of God's working in our life, family, and church.

Joseph the dreamer, as his brother referred to him, experienced obstacles and challenges, but remained consistent and thus manifested the power of God in his life. His brothers betrayed and sold him, Potiphar's wife attempted to seduce him and had him thrown into jail, his fellow prisoners abandoned and forgot about him. However, Joseph remained steadfast and consistent in his walk with God and he became second in command.

Moses refused to move without direction from God, and sought Gods' face and wisdom diligently. This was his consistent pattern. From the first encounter at the burning bush, he began the journey of harnessing the presence of God in his life. He had to wear a veil because of the greatness of Gods' glory that shone through him. God was able to use him to do tremendous things.

Ruth stayed faithful to Naomi's God and was consistent in her commitment to Naomi, she gained favour and power.

What does momentum look like in the life of a Christian?

- It is God working through us, for us, and around us.
- It shows up in the powerful preaching, the answer to prayer, and the deep connection to faith.
- It fortifies our commitment to him and His covenant to us.
- It's where God speaks to us personally. Rhema.

What are the benefits of momentum?

- Strength for the journey
- We grow from milk to meat; we can move from faith to faith and begin to believe for others
- Being steadfast we are able to stand firm on His word, as His power becomes a constant in our life.
- We find power to endure adversity and can be long suffering because we know who is carrying us
- Direction in being led by the spirit and are delivered from pitfalls of the enemy.
- He gives us power to become the sons of God and to stand in solidarity with truth.

♥ <u>The Hope</u>: Your prayer time is essential. You are building momentum.

Reflection:

1. Are you being consistent with your prayer life? What is standing in the way?

2. What can you do to enhance your prayer life?

3. Make a list of the need that are in your church and turn them into a prayer list.

4. Build your own analogy: what are some things that rely on power or force to increase in strength and momentum? Can you see a parallel to your faith? Share this with someone as an encouragement.

Challenge:

Look at the rhythm of your day. Find a space of time where you can regularly meet with God. For me, it's the wee hours of the morning, when my house is most quiet, no one needs mom, no technology is on, everyone is still asleep and the house is mine. Its also the hour when I am most alert. If possible, dedicate a space, this can be your kitchen, bathroom, or closet etc. I have used all these spaces over the years. It does not have to be large, but it would be ideal if you could lie down (for those seasons, when you need to lay prostrate before God). Small children, can learn to respect your dedicated time. Sometimes my daughter will come into the room lay down and fall asleep, at other times I just rock her while I pray. It can work. In His presence there is peace.

Write: Proverbs 18:15

Solidarity

Read: Exodus 17: 8-16
Write: Psalm 133:1-2

solidarity: is unity or agreement of feeling our action especially among individuals with a common goal

A consistent prayer life, cultivates the power that builds solidarity in the body of Christ. Once we begin to harness the presence of God in our life, we can expect to see breakthrough, deliverance, and unity. This will be the strength of the church. We are all part of the body of Christ, with integral roles. The hand cannot say to the foot, I do not need you. Likewise, we should not despise the differences and diversity of gifts, talents, and callings in the assembly. *Be kindly affectioned one to another with brotherly love; in honour preferring one another* (Romans 12:10)

We are all in this battle together, fighting the good fight of faith and wrestling against principalities and powers (Ephesians 6:12). We need the strength of unity to overcome. The children of Israel would have been defeated, in the battle against Amalek, if Moses, Aaron, and Hur did not stand together in solidarity and if Joshua was not fighting valiantly on the battlefield. This story is such a powerful example of bearing one another's burden and working together. We are not alone; we need each other to win.

What does solidarity look like in the life of a Christian?

- It's bearing one another's burden and standing together in one mind helping each other reach heaven and exalting the name of Jesus together.
- It's praying diligently for each other and endeavoring to keep the peace.
- It's practical help when someone has a need (financially, emotionally, support etc)
- It's charity

What are the benefits of solidarity?

- Knowing you are not alone
- We become rooted as one making it difficult to be moved by adversities and trials

- We become built up and abound
- We have power to fight as a unit (two are better than one, and a three-fold cord is not easily broken)
- God's favour when we are united and steadfast (Joshua and Caleb) (Nehemiah 14)

♥ <u>The Hope</u>: You were made to be connected.

Reflection:

1. What are you gifts? Talents?

2. Are you using them in the kingdom of God? If not, why? Is it fear?

3. Who is responsible for your talents? If fear is standing in you, find scriptures and begin to pray them over your life.

4. How might your talents enhance the church and be a blessing?

Challenge:

One way to deepen your bible study, is to cross examine words. This can be done by looking at the definitions, finding the synonyms and antonyms. Try cross examining the following words: consistency, momentum, and solidarity. Does this give you any new insight to the meaning of these words? Can you find these and their antonyms exemplified in the Bible? What was the outcome?

Let us fight for our families, stand with our church, our husbands, other believers. Be consistent and stand for truth in righteousness. In His presence there is sobriety.

Write: Psalm 133:1-2

At the Core

Read: Ruth 1:16-17, 2 King 20:15-27, 2 Samuel 22:2-4
Write: Ruth 2:12

A healthy relationship has a core structure that is central to its existence. Truth, trust, and trial are a few key components that come to mind. Truth creates a foundation; trials make us stronger and trust binds us together. In today's devotion, we will look at the aspect of trust.

Core; the central part of various fruits containing seeds (seeds needed for procreation, regeneration, and continued existence) or the central most important part of something

The core of the human body is described as the midsection including front, back and sides containing mainly muscles, aka the torso, it's also the body's centre of power. The muscles work as stabilizers for the entire body.

Think about the role that trust plays in your personal relationships. Imagine a marriage without trust? A parent-child relationship without trust. What would the structure be like? Weak and fraught with tension, insecurity or turmoil; lacking power. Likewise, without trust in God, we become fragile in faith and distracted, ultimately losing out with God.

♥ <u>The Hope</u>: You can fortify your relationship

You can strengthen your relationships through; intimacy (prayer – Jude 20-21), intention (focus and commitment Prov 21:5), and introspection (examining yourself and environment Lam 3:40)

Ruth trusted in God, was a worshipper, and became fruitful as a matriarch in the lineage of King David. He was also as a worshipper and a man after God's own heart. Do you see a pattern? What if Ruth followed in the footsteps of her Sister-in-Law Orpah? In contrast Gehazi (2 King 20:15-27) trusted in something else. What was his reward? What if he had fully trusted, what might have been his legacy? The more we trust God, the stronger we become. Out of that comes seed of faith, legacy, and the fruits of the spirit.

The Word says: *but without faith it is impossible to please him: For he that cometh to God must believe that he is, and that he is a rewarder of them that diligently seek him.* Hebrews 11:6. Our faith in God is rooted in our ability to trust Him; to trust that He is who He says He is. A lot of times when we face turmoil, we can question Him and falter. This is part of the trial and test that makes us stronger and draws us closer; if we allow it to. In His presence there is an anchor.

Reflection:

1. What has been testing the core and parameters of your relationships with Jesus Christ?

2. Does your relationship with God affect your relationship with others?

3. If you are facing a trial, what do you think that God wants you to learn or walk away with?

Challenge:

In your time of reflection and prayer, take a closer look at the things that gnaw away at the core of your relationship with God or attempt to undermine your faith in Him. Cast them down and begin to strengthen your core. Now reflect on your relationship with others. Take time to pray for them. If you know anyone that is having a difficult time in their own relationships, add this to your prayer list.

Dig Deeper:

 Use this devotional as a launching place for digging further. Try a topical bible study on trust.

~ 92 ~

Write: Ruth 2:12

Jehovah Rapha

Read: Exodus 15, Psalm 103:3, Psalm 147:6
Write: Psalm 147:6

Water is a reflective surface, especially when still. I remember walking around Loafers Lake and seeing the trees reflected in the water, the image was picture perfect, if you stared long enough, you could not make out the line between the water and the earth, it seemed to appear as one.

Water is significant throughout the bible and there is so much symbolism and truth that can be identified and extracted from this one word. At times, it represents life, healing, or the Word of God. With a body of water, one has the opportunity to see their image perfectly as if looking into a mirror.

Consider the children of Israel as they were at the waters of Marah. They came to a place where they were confronted with bitter water. It's not until after they cry out that the Lord turns the water into something sweet. This story is somewhat paralleled with Jesus' miracle of the wine at the wedding feast. He takes plain water and turns it into fine wine. But first, the need has to be expressed (John 2:1-11). What might the Lord have wanted the children of Israel to see, especially coming out of Egypt. The chapter starts with a song of rejoicing and testimony after Israel had seen God's great power, and then a few lines later, there is murmuring in the camp. In His presence there are rivers of living water.

♥ <u>The Hope</u>: Your bitter can become sweet.

Reflection:

1. How does God identify himself? How is that demonstrated in the miracle of the water?

2. What conditions does He place on His promise? How does that parallel our walk with God today?

Challenge:

In your time of reflection and prayer, mediate on the goodness of God and His healing virtue that He has made available to you through His work on the cross.

If you are struggling with anything in your spirit, ask God to heal you, it does not matter how major or how minor the issue is. He is just and able to forgive and heal. As you pray remember those who are hurting and looking for a miracle.

Dig Deeper:

John 2:1-10. What truth can you unearth in the miracle?

James 3:11 asks" Doth a fountain send forth at the same place sweet water and bitter?" In answer to the question… No, but bitter can become sweet by the hand of the Lord

Write: Psalm 147:6

Apples of Gold in Pictures of Silver

Read: Genesis: 19:12-30
Write: Proverb 25: 11-12

I'm always on the hunt for nuggets of gold, or as proverbs says apples of gold in pictures of silver. The Lord speaks in so many ways, His means and methods are vast. Yesterday while on a walk by Lake Ontario, we spotted a large driftwood floating close to the shore about 20 feet long. It looked as though someone plucked up an entire tree and tossed it in the Lake. My husband jokingly said, "let's go canoeing," of course the kids looked at him like he was crazy. "If we were stuck in the middle of the lake with nothing, that piece of driftwood would be very valuable," my husband responded, "we'd be looking for anything to keep us afloat." This sparked a conversation on value and perspective. Sometimes, its not until with hit a crisis or are confronted with danger or death, that we truly value what is around us. Let us bring it home to today. Think about the present value of healthy eating, vitamins, or even going for a walk. How has today's current events changed your perspective?

They say that an ounce of prevention is worth more than a pound of cure. It is better to avoid danger or trouble by listening to wisdom than to fall into a trap and attempt to find rescue. The Word of God is the road map for our souls. It is the manual that was written specifically for humanity. In the bible, we can find all the truth, prevention, and value to guide our perspective through life. While we have time, we should seek the voice, word, and wisdom of God that will prepare and strengthen us for the time of trouble, catastrophe, and eternity! How can we neglect so great salvation? In His presence we are preserved.

❤ <u>The Hope</u>: You can be anchored by His wisdom.

Reflection:

1. What instructions did the angels give Lot?

2. Why was Lot afraid to follow through? What eventually happened?

3. Have you ever turned away from sound advice? How has that impacted you?

Challenge:

In your time of prayer and reflection ask, the Lord to open your eyes, ears, and heart to His Word and voice. What is one of the wisest or most edifying word that someone has shared with you? Was it a quote? An anecdote? A cautionary tale? Write it down.

Dig Deeper:

Take time to diligently study the book of Proverbs. Unearth the truth and wisdom that forms the back bone of this Book. Meditate on scripture and allow yourself time to absorb the Word. *Thy word have I hid in mine heart that I might not sin against thee. Psalm 119:11*

Beware of the Mouldy Bread!

Read: Joshua 9, John 6:32-37
Write: Jeremiah 24:7

Mouldy bread can make you sick, even inhaling the spores can stir up breathing problems. When I eat packaged bread, it makes me sick, so I have started making my own bread, and there's a huge difference in the way that my body responds to homemade bread. What is the difference? Probably the ingredients and the freshness.

League: an agreement to combine for a particular purpose.

In Joshua 9, the power of God was moving with Joshua and the Israelites God was giving them territory and authority, position, and power, which created terror in the nearby cities. In desperation, the men of Gibeon in disguise and with mouldy bread tricked Joshua into entering, league with them. Their goal was to derail God's intended plan and purpose for Israel and ultimately preserve themselves. They were successful to some measure, but ultimately Gods plan pursued. Proverbs 24:15-16 states: Lay not wait, O wicked man, against the dwelling of the righteous; spoil not his resting place: For a just man falleth seven times, and riseth up again: but the wicked shall fall into mischief.

Beware of the mouldy bread of the world that serves as a distraction from the bread of life, the fresh bread that comes down from heaven, made especially for your spiritual sustenance. Jesus is the bread of life. His Word and wisdom are more than enough to teach us and keep us and to comfort us. There are so many distractions that we can become pre-occupied with: injustices, uproars, sickness, fighting, conspiracy theories, threatenings, uncertainty, and the list goes on. The answer is in the Word of God, if only humanity would stop, look, and listen. Sure, you could probably get by with mouldy bread, but for how long and why take the risk, when there is something fresher, healthier, and purer? In His presence we are rooted.

♥ <u>The Hope</u>: You don't need to stay down.

Reflection:

1. What is trying to thwart God's purpose and power in your life?

2. What is the devil trying to give you in exchange for what God would do through you?

If you have been tricked or led astray, you can get back up.

Challenge:

Turn everything off, reduce the noise and tumult, take some time to read the Word of God. In your time of prayer and devotion, check your spiritual cupboard. What is on the shelves, what have you been eating, what are you watching, what are you listening to? How is it affecting your spiritual health? Are you feeling depressed? Despondent? Confused? Take this to the Lord in prayer. Remove anything in your cupboard that has grown stale or mouldy and replace it with the fresh bread of life. Don't just rely on good preaching and lovely music, but get into the bible, one on one with God!

Finally: *But he answered and said, It is written, Man shall not live by bread alone, but by every word that proceedeth out of the mouth of God.* Matthew 4:4

Dig Deeper:

Read Matthew 4:1-11. Reflect on Jesus' temptation. What can you learn from His example?

Write: Jeremiah 24:7

Policies and Procedures

Read: Deuteronomy 17:17-20, 2 Kings 22: 1-20,2 Timothy 2:15
Write: 2 Timothy 2:15

When I was working in finances, I would often refer to our policies and procedures, it was my main source of direction before asking questions. These were the guidelines that formed the backbone of every task, function, and decision that we made.   If an announcement was made about a change to bank policy or procedure, I would not rely on just the words of management, but I would go directly to the policies and procedures, familiarize myself with it and then implement the changes with confidence. How can we know what is expected of us, unless we go to the manual?

Sometimes I would use them like textbooks. Why? So that I could:

(1) Fully understand what was expected of me,

(2) Become an expert in executing my task, and

(3) Make good sound decisions especially when confronted with challenges.

Knowing and understanding was key to being a successful employee and team player.

Living for God is not much different; actually, I believe it was my faith and the principles of the Word of God that helped me to apply this approach to working. As a child of God, it's important for us to know the Word of God for ourselves. It will help us to stay on the right track and keep us from following deceptive interpretations. *Study to shew thyself approved unto God, a workman that needeth not to be ashamed, rightly dividing the word of truth.* 2 Timothy 2:15 knowing the Word for ourselves, will help us to make sound decisions and to pray effectively. In His presence there is truth.

♥ <u>The Hope</u>: You were made to understand the Word.

Reflection:

1. What is your take away from today's scripture reading?

2. How do you approach your bible reading?

3. What things help you to really dissect and understand the Word?

4. List (3) things that will help you to improve your approach to bible reading. Implement them.

Challenge:

If you do not have one already, create a bible reading plan for studying the bible and then follow it. You can start by creating reading goals. In your time of prayer and devotion today, ask the Lord to help you to absorb His word into your spirit and heart and to open your eyes to deeper and greater understanding.

Write: 2 Timothy 2:15

What time is it?

Read: 2 Peter 3:9, Acts 3:19, 1 John 1:9, Revelation 3:18-22, Joel 2:13, Proverbs 1:23

Write: Revelation 3:20

Emergence: the process of coming into view or becoming exposed after being concealed.

What if this is the time of emerging from our cocoons? How should we respond? As I think about the butterfly and the stages it goes through to reach the point of emergence, I am prompted to think about where the church is; both the corporate and the individual saints. Where are we in God's eternal plan for humanity. Fact: We know that He is coming again.

After going through a series of stages and changes, what started out a tiny larva becomes a pupa and goes through stages of molting, changing its outer skeleton, growing bigger and stronger each time and finally emerges as a beautiful butterfly, with an array of colours and patterns. From glory to glory! The butterfly will eventually embark on a journey of migration to a distant destination.

In recent years, a lot has happened: there has been a huge shift in dynamics on the world stage, there has been a stripping away and there has been a surfacing of deep-seated issues. What if these occurrences are an open call to repentance? Addressing all the secret and open sins and sores that have run out before God; day and night.

As we emerge from this current stage, never to be the same, no longer a larva but something different. Where will we be?

Have we molted for the last time and are we ready to enter our cocoon in preparation for emerging as a butterfly or has this been our time of cocooning, and are, we ready to embark on our journey of migration?

Truly our God is a merciful God in that He has not consumed us in His wrath, but has been longsuffering towards all humanity! In His presence there is mercy.

♥ <u>The Hope</u>: You are being prepared.

Reflection:

1. What are some of the challenges we are facing as Christians everywhere? Create a list. Write today's prayer and keep it near as a tool to help guide your prayer. Many times, we define the mission field as some far distant place; and it is that among other things; however, the mission field starts in our closet, when we pray.

Challenge:

In today's time of prayer and reflection, ask the Lord to prepare your heart and the heart of the saints across the world for His arrival and our final emergence. There is an open call to repentance, and while everything is turning upside down, if we can zero in on God's character and the way He moved throughout the Old Testament, then we can understand that there is nothing new with God but we may very well be experiencing and witnessing His grace and mercy, as He is making an open call to all humanity and preparing us for that final emergence!

Talking to Yourself

Read: Ephesians 5:17-20, 2 Kings 4: 38-41
Write: Psalms 1:3

Do you talk to yourself? When I was working in the 9 to 5 realm, I would spend a lot of time humming or singing quietly in my cubicle on the job. Many noticed and described it as calming and peaceful (which surprised me). It was a way of keeping my mind sharp and focused, especially in a very monotonous environment where the tasks were very repetitive.

During my time at Sick Kids, I spent a lot of time worshipping quietly and became known for singing. The doctors and nurses of the NICU noticed that it not only calmed my baby but all the babies seemed more restful (based on the trending oxygen saturations). It broke up the incessant sound of the beeping monitors and pumps. What motivated me? I love having the presence of God with me. There is just something about praising and worshipping the true and living God that just changes the atmosphere. His holiness is purity, his presence is life. To this day, my daughter is easily moved by worship.

When we are in places where we feel restricted, we can pause and make melodies in our heart that encourages us and changes things. We can meditate. It is like incense radiating through the atmosphere, seeping through cracks in walls and barriers to reach the throne of God. This reminds me of Elisha and the death pot (2 Kings 4: 38-41). Our worship is like the meal that was thrown into the pot, to neutralize the poison; it counters the negative attitudes, and pessimistic voices that do not know the goodness of God.

God has put His anointing in us, His vessels of clay. Pour it out throughout the day.

♥ <u>The Hope</u>: Your worship is powerful.

Reflection:

1. What worship songs inspire you to reflect on the nature of God?

2. Can you recall a time when the Lord met with you deeply during a
    season of worship?

3. Research and list some benefits of worship.

Challenge:

Today when you go about your day, encourage yourself with scripture and
song. Incorporate worship in your prayer time. Throughout the day remind,
yourself to keep the essence of praise flowing before God. If you are
feeling down, encourage yourself with a hymn. If you have not already,
make singing and worship a regular part of your quiet time with God. In
His presence there is a song.

Write: Psalms 1:3

Keep Digging

Read: Genesis 26: 1-25, Psalms 37, Proverbs 5:15-17
Write: Proverbs 10:11

Most civilizations started near a water source. Sometime ago I had an opportunity to look at a population density map during a geography lesson with my kids, there were many camps near the water sources, both inland or coastal. Water is needed to: sustain life, maintain livestock, grow food, travel, and cleaning, these are just a few reasons. The water is essential for prosperity, because without it things die. There were rivers that flowed out of Eden (Gen 2:10-11). Where you find water, you will usually find life teeming in and around it.

Let's pause and think about Isaacs's journey through this passage of Scripture.

God gives Isaac a word of direction and a promise, he obeys, then faces opposition and strife, but continues relentlessly until he gets the breakthrough. Finally, God meets him to comfort and reaffirm the promise. Isaac who is our example, did not give up, he kept digging. Jesus said that if we believe in Him as the scripture says, out of our bellies will flow living water, that is the Holy Ghost, and even with the Holy Ghost there are so many things that would try to stop up the well or curb the flow. The devil, cares of life, or people who do not understand your commitment. Keep digging that well! As the word promises, we will draw from the wells of salvation with joy. We have a joy unspeakable and full of glory that the world cannot understand. So, when we are cast down look up to JESUS, continue to dig through prayer, fasting and faithfulness, because we have a promise that living waters will flow, and when the living water flows the promises of God the comfort of His word will be there to keep us moving forward.

Protect your well and do not let anything contaminate it. Your well is the lifeline to God. It sustains you, nourishes you, and maintains everything that pertains to you. In His presence there is tenacity.

♥ <u>The Hope</u>: Your well is worth fighting for.

We have many adversaries, many are the afflictions of the righteous, but the Lord delivers out of them all. It is also written that the steps of a good man is ordered by the Lord. How can we fail with His leading?

Reflection:

1. Why did the men strive with Isaac for His well? Look at verse 13-14

2. Who did they think they were fighting? Who were they really fighting with? How do you know?
   Fret not thyself because of evildoers, neither be thou envious against the workers of iniquity. Ps 37:1

Challenge:

Spend time digging your well through prayer and meditation in the Word. Fight the distractions. Examine and sift through anything that would attempt to stop up your well. Fear, weariness, peoples' opinions, tactics of the devil, or stagnation are things that the enemy throws into your well to destroy your prosperity.

Home

Read: John 14: 9-27, Psalms 91 and 19
Write: John 14:23

Home: the place where one lives. Dwelling place, domicile, abode.

Home! "There is no place like home!" ..... "Home is where the heart is!" are well known quotes that capture the essence of longing for home or returning from a long journey. Great excursions and escapades, exciting travel, and adventures, pale in comparison to coming home to the place where you find; safety, peace, love and comfort...and clean clothes.

When I found Jesus, or rather when He found me, His entrance into my life was a spectacular event. My vocabulary is limited to truly describe that first encounter. My heart was quite empty, unclean and unkempt. I was lonely and desperate! To find Him was to find home.

I remember travelling to Nigeria on a mission trip, which was truly a trip of a life time. It was a wonderful experience that I will never forget. Christ was there, new friends and fellowship, however when it was time to come home; there was a longing to see my husband, hug my children, and worship with my church family. There is something precious about finding a place of comfort, where the worries remain on the peripheral and the warm of the familiar holds you tight.

The time I spent living downtown Toronto to be near Sick Kids was a temporary relief and distraction during a family crisis; delayed responsibility, meals provided, away from mundane routine and pressures. During this time the Lord really provided for my family and I. Christ was there in Toronto, but the time came I was more than ready to go home and return to normal life. I longed to be home; that place of safety and insulation. These experiences taught me that Christ is home. Wherever He is, there is safety, security, warmth, and love.

For us as believers, Christ is home. When we let Jesus fill the temple of our hearts, there's a fire that continues through darkness, periods of sadness, loneliness and uncertainty, and leads us to the place of solace, wisdom, and understanding. In His presence there is warmth and connection.

♥ <u>The Hope</u>: Your home is in Christ

2 Cor:1: 3-5

Blessed be God, even the Father of our Lord Jesus Christ, the Father of mercies, and the God of all comfort;

Who comforteth us in all our tribulation, that we may be able to comfort them which are in any trouble, by the comfort wherewith we ourselves are comforted of God.

For as the sufferings of Christ abound in us, so our consolation also aboundeth by Christ.

Reflection:

1. How would you describe home? What does it mean to you to be home in Christ?

Challenge:

As you spend time in your home, decorate your house with praise, thanksgiving, and worship. Enjoy His presence and take time, listen to His words, which leads to peace and comfort. Let your temple be filled with His wonder and majesty. He is the Interior Designer and knows exactly what you need.

Dig Deeper:

Complete a topical study on the words: abode and dwelling. Find a hymn on the topic of "anchor", what are the parallels to the Christian life and relationship with Jesus Christ.

Write: John 14:23

Relationships

Read: Mark 12:30-31, Galatians 5:14-26, Proverbs 27:17
Write: Proverbs 27:17

This morning I woke up with a simple thought in mind, our relationships are the only important things that we can take with us into eternity and from day to day. Each day is an opportunity to build stronger and better relationships with God, and with others. Health may fail, finances may fail, but lasting relationships built with care and love on the solid principles of the Word of God will stand the test of failure and adversity, and buoy us up during times of troubled seas.

Did you know that oftentimes the Lord strategically places people in your life, according to His will and purpose for your life?

Think about your parents, siblings, husband. They challenge us and our faith in different ways, but God uses these people and circumstances to shape us. After all He is the Potter!

What is the temperature like in your relationships? I know that there are some things that we cannot control, but what about in areas where we can have influence? Several people in the bible invested time and care in building healthy relationships, not knowing how it would turn out. As a result, there were rewards, comfort, and deliverance in the time of need.

Naomi and Ruth, are a great duo, there is so much we can learn from them. They built a unique and special relationship. Through this union Naomi gains comfort and companionship, Ruth gains a wise counsellor, advocate, and friend.

The Shunammite woman, who built a room for the prophet Elisha, also had a unique relationship, which was faithful and different. Through this relationship her son was restored to life, and the prophet had a place to stay with an extended family. I can imagine that a prophet travelling often could be burdensome at times. When I travelled to Nigeria, the hospitality and accommodations made me feel welcomed. Later this woman's land was restored, all as a result of her relationship with Elisha.

How about David and Jonathan? The bible says that their souls were knit together. They found a confidant in each other. Mephibosheth, Jonathan's son, was a recipient of grace and love borne out of their relationship and had security, while David had a comfort and constant reminder of his good friend.

And finally, Abraham was called a friend of God.

♥ <u>The Hope</u>: You are a friend of God.

The relationships that we are careful to build today, can become towers of refuge for us tomorrow. In His presence there is love.

Reflection:

1. How important are your earthly relationships to you?

2. Do any need improvement?

3. How might you help those relationships to move forward with grace?

Challenge:

Seek to establish quality time with God, verses quantity. We meet often as a body of believers and as a result we establish quantity time with JESUS. But what about quality time, where you speak, He hears, He speaks and you listen intently, friend to friend and face to face?

 Think about your own personal relationships, there are times when I need to be alone with my husband, and at other times we are surrounded by friends. In your time of prayer, ask the Lord to help you to be faithful in your relationships with others and how to apply a soft answer or to be the iron that they need. May you be a blessing to someone else!

Write: Proverbs 27:17

The Little Pepper

Read: Judges 11: 1-33
Write: 1 Cor 3:7

I recall strolling outside with my husband one late summer evening, admiring his vegetable garden. His crop was springing up quite beautifully. I had watched him diligently tend to his garden visiting everyday at varying times, sometimes early in the morning, mid afternoon, late evening or just before sunset, usually watering in the cool of the evening to prepare them for the following day. He gets so excited farming and reaping his handiwork. As we were out there, he was admiring the callaloo, he has two beds of callaloo, one is east facing and the other north facing. The eastern bed, had a weak start and faced some scorching in the beginning. But they prevailed against the elements and became tall, green, and luscious. Next, he marvelled at his pepper plant, "my Lise, I can't believe my little pepper tree grew, it really surprised me." He did not have much hope for the little pepper tree, because it also did not have the best start. He planted by faith, eyed it cautiously, and did not hold the highest expectations. We have since eaten it and I can say that it was so spicy and nice. It is interesting the life lessons we can learn through a simple vegetable garden.

As I thought about the little pepper tree and the crop of weak callaloo, I reflected on how we sometimes lose hope and our faith grows weary when things do not materialize the way we expect it to or when the answers to our prayer seem so delayed. It can be really trying. We have an Everlasting God; whose hands are not short. He is like the faithful farmer, watching us and the circumstances that affect us. He makes His presence known at different times always watering the seeds of faith in us at just the right moment.

♥ <u>The Hope</u>: You have an Everlasting God.

1 Corinthians 13:7 speaking of charity says it: Beareth all things, believeth all things, hopeth all things, endureth all things

There are seeds that the Lord is planting in you and in the people around you little by little day by day. The Lord through His love and patience is working in our lives, the lives of the people that we live with, the lives of those we care for, and the lives of those we meet. Do not give up hope, keep praying, and believing, remembering the little pepper, that when it finally bore fruit, not only provided joy from its mere presence in the garden, but also added flavour to the pot and joy to the lips.

Think about Sarah, whose dead womb brought forth fruit or little David who appeared weak in the shadow of his brothers. These through great adversity and great triumph, broke through to change the world around them. In His presence there is survival.

Reflection:

1.   Why was Jephthah despised among his brethren and how did they perceive him?

2.   What do you find interesting about his journey? Can you relate?

3.   Create a word map for the word "weak".

Challenge:

 Who or what is the little pepper in your life today? In your time of prayer and devotion today, lift it up before the Lord, with intention, focus, and renewed faith. Trust that where you are weak, He will not only water, but He will cause life and success.

Dig Deeper:

In your time of reflection, think back to a situation in the bible that parallels the story of the Little Pepper, pick one and spend time reading it, allow it to be a launching point for deeper conversation with God.

Write: 1 Cor 3:7

Be Cleaned

Read: Lev 14:1-8, Leviticus 15: 31, Psalm 51, Luke 8:43-48,1 John 1:7-9
Write: John 1:17

Over the past weeks I have started reading the book of Leviticus. It speaks of sacrificial offerings and the priests. God clearly outlined what was unclean or clean, and the process for purification. In the Old Testament, no unclean thing could come before a Holy God, it would be destroyed. Consider Phineas and Hophni, who were killed inside the tabernacle, because they brought strange fire into the presence of God. Judgement executed instantaneously. However, when our Lord, Jesus Christ came to earth in flesh, he dwelt among the unclean and brought wholeness and healing. The cleansings offered under the law were temporary and needed to be done ritually; and judgement was exacted through death. In contrast, Jesus' sacrifice and blood is the offering that was done once and for all and through Him we have the hope of eternity.

"Not by works of righteousness which we have done, but according to his mercy he saved us, by the washing of regeneration, and renewing of the Holy Ghost; Which he shed on us abundantly through Jesus Christ our Saviour;" (Titus 3:5-6) I am thankful for Jesus and his cleansing blood. We no longer need to shed the blood of pigeons and lambs because his blood is enough. In His presence there is salvation.

❤ <u>The Hope</u>: Your salvation has been wrought by Jesus

Reflection:

1. Read 1 Corinthians 6:9-11 and reflect on how this relates to the cleansing required in the Old Testament.

2. The bible teaches that faith without works is dead. Have you ever
    felt pressure to earn or maintain your salvation through works
    only? How did you deal with that disconnect? Or to maintain your
    salvation through faith only? How do faith and works manifest in
    your life?

3. What does it mean to you to be saved?

Write: John 1:17

Halloween: A Day to Rejoice *(Testimony)*

Read: Psalm 71
Write: Psalms 71:15-16

October 31st is Halloween Day , celebrated mainly North American as a tradition. I don't celebrate the festivities around Halloween, but it is a memorable day for me. At work I used to decline the candy offers from my coworkers, the understood that I didn't practice the tradition. However, I would tell them that I celebrate "Hallowed Eve"; the puzzled expressions on their faces were always funny. You see, 21 years ago, I was baptized in the wonderful name of JESUS and filled with the baptism of the Holy Ghost. On the day when many were celebrating the dead, I was saved from death and brought to life. My life was on a very dark path of depression and dysfunction. I was literally a lost soul, and I would not be here today, as a mother of 4, married and enjoying life. Surely, He makes the barren woman to rejoice and be a mother of children. JESUS saves lives.

Back to my story, early Sunday morning on October 31st, 1999, my brother called me to pick him up from a club located downtown Toronto; he had gotten stranded after an all-nighter. We made it safely downtown, but on my way back my car engine caught on fire and had to be towed. I was desperately waiting to get to the evening service, and this was an attack, I knew the devil was on my tail. Up until this point I had been in a spiritual battle and I thought I was days away from death. My mind was so far gone. I was afraid to sleep and had not slept in over 72 hours. Several times I sat down to write a letter to my parents to explain how I had died in my sleep, but kept telling myself, this was not the way I was supposed to go. On October 30th "Devils night" I was extremely fearful and exhausted, I could hear pounding on my walls, and every time I nodded off to sleep, I would feel a spirit oppressing me. Exhausted, I called the only Christians that I knew late in the night, a young couple who were Seventh Day Adventist and Carlton, my son's father, who was newly confessing a faith in JESUS, we had been estranged for several years and were not together at the time. We gathered in a circle, holding hand and they prayed form. After they, left I stayed up the whole night waiting for daybreak to rise on Sunday. The nights were tortuous. When my car caught on fire that morning the level of fear increased. Fast forward to Sunday evening

~ 125 ~

service and I was stood shaking with absolute dread. The message was preached and I was broken. I ran to the altar with my 5-year-old son, wept over my sins and poured out my heart, dear "Sister Eve" whispered in my ears "Jesus wants to know if you would like to take His name on in water baptism". With no hesitation, my response was yes. I need to be free.

While I was in the baptismal tank surrounded by the warm water, I heard the Lord say this is my blood. It was the most refreshing and liberating experience. I knew JESUS was with me. But I also knew that I needed more power to fight the demons that were after me. I could not go home without the power. I was so desperate. Once the baptism was over, and the service was ending, I felt still nervous and unequipped. As I stood in the back row of the church my heart reached out to God and He filled me with the baptism of the Holy Ghost. It was powerful, rivers of living water began to flow as I spoke in tongues for the first time. Finally, I was ready to go home. I will never forget that Hallowed Eve way back in 1999. It is the day that JESUS sanctified me and became King of my life forever.

This is not so much a devotional as it is an invitation to stroll with me down memory lane and remember the goodness of God. All my life He has been faithful and all my life He has been oh so good and with every breath that I am able, I want to praise Him!! In His presence there is deliverance.

♥ <u>The Hope</u>: Your testimony is powerful.

Reflection:

1.   What is your salvation story? Write it down.

Challenge

As you seek the Lord today, remember the goodness of God in your life. Think back to where He first spoke to you. For me it was in the baptismal tank. Think about the moment He filled you with His spirit and bask in His goodness. He is the same yesterday, today, and forever. Share your story with someone, who has not heard it.

Dear *Woman of God,*

I hope that these devotions have set you on the path of building your relationship with God and getting to know His word.

We live in a day and age where technology has become an important part of the things that we do. This along with life and responsibilities competes for our attention. I encourage you to keep digging deeper.

Thank you for taking the time to journey with me, through these devotions. It has been a blessing to write and share the hope that I have found in Jesus Christ. I have learned that trials, patience, and experiences provide the rich soil in which a vibrant hope and faith can grow. It is the place where testimonies are formed.

Cultivating More Patience Experience Hope (Volume 2) will be coming out soon with more devotions, challenges, and reflections to help you to continue this journey. Stay tuned for this upcoming project.

I would love to hear your feedback. Please feel free to reach out at mslise@lisasimoneadamson.com. You can also sign up for notifications on new and upcoming projects at www.lisasimoneadamson.com.

The Lord bless thee, and keep thee: The Lord make his face shine upon thee, and be gracious unto thee:The Lord lift up his countenance upon thee, and give thee peace. Numbers 6:24-26

Faith, Light & Love,

Ms. Lise

Notes:

Notes: